ROADSIDE BICYCLE REPAIR

A POCKET MANIFESTO

BY SAM TRACY

speck press

golden

Published by Speck Press
An imprint of Fulcrum Publishing
4690 Table Mountain Drive • Suite 100 • Golden, Colorado 80403 • speckpress.com

© 2008 Sam Tracy

ISBN-13: 978-1-933108-18-6

This publication is provided for informational and educational purposes. The information herein contained is true and complete to the best of our knowledge.

Library of Congress Cataloging-in-Publication Data

Tracy, Sam.
  Roadside bicycle repair : a pocket manifesto / by Sam Tracy.
     p. cm.
  Includes bibliographical references and index.
  ISBN 978-1-933108-18-6 (pbk.)
 1. Bicycles--Maintenance and repair--Amateurs' manuals. 2. Bicycling.
I. Title.

TL430.T732 2008
629.28'772--dc22

                              2007051841

10 9 8 7 6 5 4 3 2

Book layout and design by Margaret McCullough
Printed on recycled paper in Canada by Friesens Corp.
Pages 4, 9, 19, 50, 79, 92, 106, 114, 120 images courtesy © Comstock, page 88, 37 © iStock, page 62 © Kim Reece.
All other photos provided by © Sam Tracy and © Kerri Spindler-Ranta.

Acknowledgments

I'd like to thank the good folks at Speck Press for fielding and feeding the pocket book idea, my lovely wife Kerri for getting the pictures, and all my friends at HomeStart in Boston, not least for the peace to write through my lunch hours.

The soundtrack to this book includes Gogol Bordello, Kill Your Idols, Fela Kuti, Mu, Battalion of Saints, Detroit Cobras, Agent Orange, Laibach, Suicide Commandos, Quincy Punks, Atmosphere, Sage Francis, Asian Dub Foundation, New Order, Upright Citizens, Khaled's *Kenza*, Wagram's *Oriental Fever*, WMBR-Cambridge, and WZBC-Boston.

TABLE OF CONTENTS

Introduction   7

1: Flight Check   11

2: Wheels   15

3: Seats & Seatposts   43

4: Handlebars & Stems   51

5: Brakes   63

6: Drivetrains   89

References   107

Index   115

INTRODUCTION

This is freedom: you're on your bike, pedaling through whatever comes to pass, shooting your way past blocks of gridlock and overcrowded buses, chasing and improvising through a course of your own design. And you leave no trace but the experience itself...*nothing like the present.*

Some drivers don't appreciate the candor of your choices, instead tossing petty obstacles in your path—the suddenly opened car door, the unplanned lane change, the sheer oblivion of a sorely truncated worldview—but theirs is a dying culture; its petulant gestures merit nothing more than a reflexive response. The bicycle's own contributions will inevitably supercede, mingling with the passing world to define the texture of your ride.

This freedom, unlike the oil supply, is worthy of our defense. You do face the prospects of the inexorable flats, crashes, and breaks while riding your bike. But these are only passing dilemmas, for the simple truth is that bike repair is accessible, and this is *the* book for bikes on the move. You'll only need the foresight to make rudimentary preparations.

Roadside Bicycle Repair means to complement a small assortment of portable tools—a patch kit, some tire levers, and a pump; one of those clever metric Allen- and socket-wrench sets from your favorite local bike shop; a screwdriver and perhaps an adjustable wrench—but the truly dedicated might also pack spare tubes, a spoke wrench, and a chain tool with extra links. Throw it all in an old sock, which also doubles as a handy rag. The collection might seem cumbersome, but really it's no more than an extra lunch. The toolbox on my bench weighs ninety pounds; you'll do just fine. Note that some older bikes may require less common implements, as described herein; the distance-minded rider will do well to peruse this volume prior to departure.

1: FLIGHT CHECK

The best way to avoid breaking down is to start out with a healthy bicycle. So much hassle can be avoided with the barest sprinkling of foresight! We can elude the pressing everyday menace of the pinch flats, to take one famous example, by ensuring the tires are fully aired in the first place. The correct measure of air pressure is noted as psi or bar at some point on the tires' sidewalls. Guesswork yields dubious results; use a pump with a gauge.

A truly roadworthy bike should further pass a basic pop quiz. To begin, the brake levers should never bottom out on the handlebars, no matter how hard you squeeze them. Ease up on the rear brake and rock the bike back and forth: Does the fork seem loose

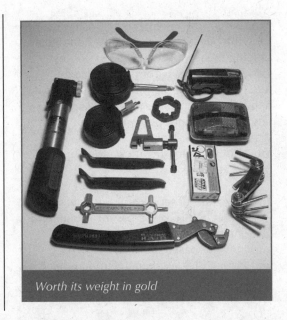

Worth its weight in gold

in the frame? You'll want to tighten the headset. Are the wheels attached securely? Do they hit the brakes or anything else when spun?

Face the bike and step up to its handlebars, bracing the front tire between your feet. Can the bars move from side to side independently of the fork? If your bike runs handlebar extensions, will they support your weight? Sloppy steering can really wreck the party. Neither should the seat move around, nor any racks, toe clips, or bottle cages.

The drivetrain deserves at least a cursory inspection before you cross the Serengeti. The chain should *barely* be damp with a quality gel-based lubricant, which will keep it cleaner than anything else. Backpedal the chain through a rag to wipe away any excess (unless you want it all

Nothing you'd want to carry around

over your legs as well) and keep an eye
out for any tight chain links. Does the
chain skip out of place around the cogs or
derailleur pulleys when backpedaling?
Sort any of this out before you set sail.

The shifting itself is best adjusted with the
aid of test rides, as we'll see, but you'll
want to be sure the components involved
are at least set up correctly before you go.
Any loose pedals or cranks? Either means to
spin in a perfect circle, without any lateral
play. If nothing else, riding loose parts
surely compounds their damage.

2: WHEELS

If there are any among us who haven't yet been afflicted with flat tires, they are here advised to remain silent about their strange fortune, lest balance return and the unspeakable intervene. Minneapolis messenger lore suggests that flats come in threes, but the first will make the point.

The nefarious spike will have attacked the rear tire, most likely, by virtue of the weight it bears. A small clique of frames and forks are strong enough to brace the wheels with only one side, and you'll want to be cautious about detaching control cables from the fourteen-speed internal hubs, but most often you'll need to remove the wheel from the frame.

First, shift the chain all the way down to the smallest cogs in front and back. Release any brakes associated with the wounded wheel, as described on pages 67 through 72, and either find a way to temporarily elevate the wheel—balancing the stem's nose atop a fence, perhaps, or through a belt strung down from a branch above— or flip the bike upside down. Loosen the wheel's skewer or locknuts and anything else attaching it to the frame.

Front wheels are indeed simpler, but the chain and derailleur out back are accommodated easily enough. Grip the foremost derailleur pulley across its axis, and pull it back away from the cogs:

REMOVING A REAR WHEEL

1: Open the brake's quick-release

2: Loosen the wheel skewer

3: Pull derailleur cage back away from axle

4: Lift wheel out of frame

the chain will open into an oblong box as the derailleur's cage straightens out, allowing for simpler wheel extraction.

Loosen the inner tube's valve—by unscrewing and briefly depressing the trim Presta valve's tip, or by pressing something small and hard to the button inside your wider Schrader valve—and roll the wheel a bit to release a little more of the tube's remaining air. This will allow your fingers the room to ease each of the tire's beads away from the rim, all the way around on each side, which in turn opens a gap for the tire levers. Install these an inch apart, and hook one to a spoke before pulling the other along the rim.

Remove the inner tube from the tire, and use your fingers and thumbs to check its tread for debris. Dig out anything you find. Any big rips? See pages 24 through 25.

You'll need a patch kit if you don't have a spare inner tube. Reinflate the original nice and big, and run it past your ear until you hear the hiss of air. You might dunk it underwater and look for the bubbles, alternately, if the opportunity presents itself. This done, let the air out again and see to it that the area right around the hole is clean, dry, and lying pretty well flat. Dose at least a patch-sized puddle of glue onto this sunny plateau and let it fully dry—tacky to the touch, not slick—before removing the foil backing and pressing the patch firmly into position.

Fit one of the tire's beads back around the rim and put a little air back in the inner tube, just enough to fill it out. You might line up the label on the tire with the rim's valve hole to provide a reference point the next time you're hunting for a sliver of glass or a tiny hole. Make sure the wheel's rim strip fully covers any spokes or spoke holes before reinstalling the tube, beginning with the valve. Scoot the installed bead over to the far side of the wheel, all the way around, before starting on the other bead. Start again at the valve, working around in both directions.

The tires are meant to fit their rims quite tightly. Your fingers may even begin to strain toward the very end. They might even wish for some tire levers to help them along, but deny them you must because the tire levers themselves are really not so clever. They'll only pinch the tube against the rim, misused in this manner, and pop it open all over again.

Nudge the installed bead to the rim's center instead, all the way around. This region almost inevitably features a shallow valley, the lower reaches of which allow *just* enough elbowroom to tip the other

FIXING A FLAT TIRE

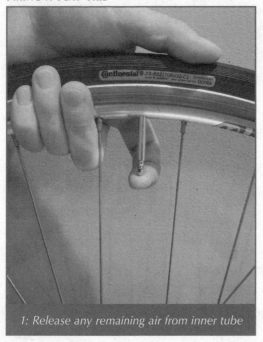

1: Release any remaining air from inner tube

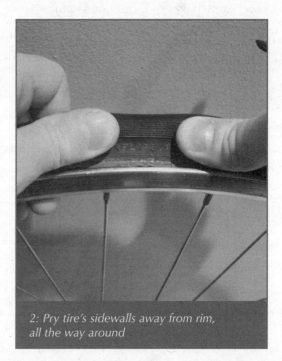

2: Pry tire's sidewalls away from rim, all the way around

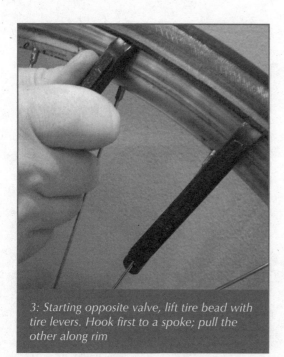

3: *Starting opposite valve, lift tire bead with tire levers. Hook first to a spoke; pull the other along rim*

4: *Check the tire thoroughly for debris*

FIXING A FLAT TIRE (CONT.)

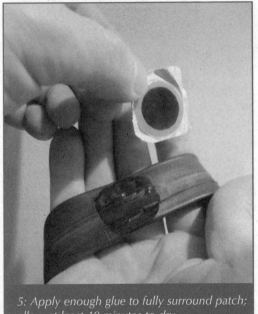

5: Apply enough glue to fully surround patch; allow at least 10 minutes to dry

6: Press patch firmly into place, especially around the edges

7: Reinflate tube just enough to make it fully round; reinstall to tire

8: Tilt tire beads back into rim, working outward from valve. Use fingers only, to avoid pinching tube

bead into place. And your fingers will be so much stronger for the effort! They might even learn to play the piano after all of this.

Make sure the beads retain a uniform position around the rim as you reinflate the tire. Start out with the wheel lying flat on the ground. You should be able to wriggle the tire around to resolve any discrepancies, up to about 20 psi.

If your brakes don't have quick-release features, reinstall the wheel to the bike before fully inflating the tube. With derailleur systems, you'll go back in the same way you came out: pull the rear derailleur cage back to make for the oblong box, and wrap the chain once again around the smallest cogs.

Beyond air pressure, your luck with the flat is principally a function of your tires.

Treads reinforced with Kevlar, or a similar material, are definitely the best option; neither retrofitted tire liners nor liquid tube sealants will fully redeem cracked or worn-out tires.

The tiny pinpricks associated with the majority of flat tires are themselves nothing to worry about—think double jeopardy or lightning striking twice—but any discernible rips should always be addressed, espeically on the sidewalls especially. The curious and excitable inner tube tries to force its way out, widening the way as it goes; bad things tend to happen.

Now, remove the tire and install a boot to its interior, thoroughly covering any damages. The classic tire boot is only a couple pieces of nice and thick Velox rim tape, overlapped to form a strong barrier, but a little cardstock under some duct tape

Tire boots: use doubled-up Velox rim tape or cardboard-reinforced duct tape

works just as well. So hang on to the roll's remainder next time you tape a rim, or mount what you need on a scrap of wax paper and throw it in your kit. Failing these, your only option might be the expensive one. Fold up a dollar bill and wedge it between the tire and a partially inflated inner tube. If your bike features generator-driven lights, move any tire boots to the side farthest from the dynamo.

Don't ride a bike with a loose wheel. It may only fall away from the bike's centerline and rub at the brake pads, if you're lucky; but it can well take you down if you're not.

Sloppy adjustments will sometimes cause a hub's bearings to loosen, but a broader misunderstanding more often leaves the wheels themselves loose within their forks and frames. The quick-release axle skewers have become all too ubiquitous in our modern world, but appreciation of their operation have come along somewhat more grudgingly, I have to say.

The quick-release lever passes through a hollow axle, compressing the frame or fork dropouts around the hub. It operates by means of a cam mechanism, which all too often is mistaken for a mere screw. Winding it tight won't keep the wheel in place! Of its two end pieces, only the *smaller* is tightened in a circle. The lever opposite is rotated in an arc, perpendicular to the wheel.

Once the wheel is in position—fully installed into the dropouts, perfectly centered in relation to the frame—you'll adjust the small end piece until the lever is tight enough, before closing the lever to secure the wheel. You should always use the palm of your hand to press the lever closed; anything else is not safe. A quick-release

Tightening a quick-release skewer

lever closed with the fingertips will not reliably hold its position. (Conversely, you'll also want to avoid the use of overbearing force, lest you strip out the skewer's wee threads.)

Bolt-on skewers have no use for cams; you'll tighten them with a 5-mm Allen key. Still other hubs incorporate bolts installed to either axle end: as with the clunky old locknuts, these should become as tight as an adult can reasonably make them.

The judiciously mounted wheel leaves us better positioned to evaluate other issues that might arise. There should never be any lateral play with the wheels. Using the frame or fork as your gauge, you should not be able to move the rim side-to-side at all. Lateral give indicates a loose hub. You don't want to be seated above such an axis, as its liberties may challenge the bike's handling. Riding them loose also destroys the hubs' working parts.

There is rarely anything to be done for loose hubs, on the road at least. Nearly all require at least one ultrathin cone wrench for adjustments; mobile repair kits tend not to include such implements. Cone wrenches arrive in half a dozen sizes, with few other purposes. You'll probably need to remove the gears as well, before adjusting the rear hub—yet more special tools—and this says nothing of any bearings, grease, or cones the hubs may require. Remember my ninety-pound toolbox? *Check things out before you go.*

Hubs sometimes become too tight as well, for the same sorts of sloppy reasons, but you probably will not know about it unless you check. The axle will spin only grudgingly, rolled with the fingers. More so than with other components, the hubs' limited servicing options present distance-minded riders with a compelling rationale for securing quality equipment in the first place.

Rims orbiting loose hubs commonly effect a drunken wobble, colliding with the brake pads at their leisure. Absent the loose hub, such testimony indicates a wheel that has lost its way. This happens often enough, bumping down the dusty road, but the condition is rarely permanent. You'll need to true the wheel.

The bicycle wheel's intrepid design leaves us some wriggle room in that we can usually make things right again with adjustments to the spoke tension. A wheel's form and strength are both functions of this measure. Flip the bike upside down, such that its wheels might spin freely given the cure.

The essentials: Craftsman adjustable wrench, tire levers, spoke wrench, and multitools

Proper wheels are built in truing stands, with spoke tensiometers and good lighting, and their injured kin are best redeemed in similar circumstances. But with only the spoke wrenches—the smallest of tools— we're *usually* able to return their circles to at least a basic accuracy. (Many of the new space-age composite wheels are trued only by the cryptic xenon twilight of their alien home worlds; but their everyday peers at least lend us a fighting chance.)

The spoke nipples are fashioned of softer metals like brass or aluminum, in obsequious deference to the impassive steel spokes they worship, and most grip their charges quite tightly. Professional wheelwrights enlist various thread-locking compounds in their arts to better guard the spoke tension against riding's ceaseless vibrations, but many more wheels inevitably succumb to the simpler persuasions of age and rust. We expect to encounter difficulties adjusting the spokes, in other words, and it will always be counterproductive to try and force the point. Old and brittle spokes sometimes snap under the pressure. (We need pliers to hold the spoke whilst turning its nipple, with the truly hard cases. On the road, we might instead ask the unruly spoke's immediate neighbors to compensate. Keep reading.)

Make sure you're using the right tool. Almost all spoke nipples arrive in one of three common sizes, and the wiser mobile-repair kits provide for three corresponding sockets. You'll want to use the socket most inclined toward those nipples you're playing with; go for the tightest fit. Outsized examples quickly strip their targets of useful features, leaving them deaf to further suggestions.

Healthy wheels enjoy uniformly high levels of spoke tension. The angles required often cause the drive-side spokes to become tighter yet. The tensiometer's correct reading is not easily described with mere words; suffice it here to say, the spokes should only *barely* move when squeezed together.

Everything from simple vibrations to jarring impacts can cause spokes to loosen individually or in groups, and this inevitably confronts the rim's profile. Squeeze the spokes in pairs all the way around: Do any seem exceptionally loose or unusually tight? We want to begin with these.

On the road, use a bike's brake pads as the reference points. (A rougher estimate might be pursued within the frame's chainstays, absent rim-mounted brakes.) Our goal is to make the rim sail smoothly through our Straits of Gibraltar, once spun.

A wheel's truing should *make sense*, in the ideal. Those spokes in need of tightening should be loose already and vice versa. Departures from this rhythm suggest a rim bent beyond redemption. Our initial focus on conspicuously loose or tight spokes, in other words, should correspond with the wheel's biggest problems.

If a rim bows to the right, we should first address the spoke(s) immediately above the bend. Those on the left can be tightened and/or those on the right can be loosened, bearing in mind that we like the spoke tension across each side to become as even as possible.

Make adjustments to the spoke nipples in minor half-turn increments, checking the results of your work at every turn. Applied successively to a rim's diminishing deviations, our measured corrections should return it to health. Truing is a dynamic process, and changes in spoke tension are registered in several directions at once, so it is possible that new issues might also emerge through the course of our efforts. The process is forward, if not always linear.

That's the crux of it. Truing does not comprise random variables; it's all about identifying specific problems and gradually correcting them. Take advantage of what light you have, and if you do come across a spoke that won't be loosened, see if you can *tighten* those spokes immediately opposite. This departs from the orthodoxy we like to pursue with the wheels, and typically impresses a temporary flat spot upon the rim, but the effort might also make your wheel just round enough to roll on home. (Hops and flat spots each confront a wheel's long-term

prospects—you want to fully resolve either at the earliest opportunity—but they're best addressed in a truing stand. Those minor enough for repair won't keep us from continuing.)

The wrong sorts of leverage—delivered with crash landings, for example—will surpass the spokes' capacities for redemption, deforming the underlying contours of the rim itself. We'll see a particularly acute bend, or perhaps a really bad flat spot. Yet spoke tension that is simply uneven can cast frighteningly long shadows; you might be surprised to learn how much good a few minutes' truing can do. You should always try, until you come to recognize dead wheels by sight.

Those taco chips unimpressed with your best efforts might only be helped with impact adjustments. Determine which way you'd like the rim to move, bring the wheel up over your head, and smash it down accordingly. This method comprises the antithesis of scientific acumen, for which we provide no guarantees, but if *nothing* else works you might give it a shot.

Broken Spokes

We only sometimes hear the broken spoke's sorrowful and distinct parting *ping* (absent the ubiquitous traffic noise), but the rhythmic and tedious rubbing that follows is difficult to ignore. It's positively cataclysmic from the brakes' perspective: the effortlessly smooth rim suddenly slams into the pads before roughly shoving them aside to take another pass.

Spokes are not supposed to break—at all. If you lose three or more, it's safe to assume that you need a stronger wheel for your purposes. The old thirty-six-spoke standard served bicycle wheels for decades, and so it should be no surprise that modern race wheels, with twenty or twenty-four spokes, prove less hardy. But regardless of spoke count, we never really see a broken spoke coming. I was quite surprised when my fancy Sapim spokes started popping around Boston, less than two years after I'd built their wheelset; but then again, my commutes are adventurous and the roads are bad.

Those spokes that do fail typically stage abrupt and solitary suicides. Losing several at once—as when a poorly adjusted rear derailleur allows the bike's chain to massacre whole rows—is even more dramatic. (You'll probably walk away from such episodes; the jury-rig described here is meant more for individual failures.) You always want to first determine which spokes are actually broken or merely loose by squeezing them together in pairs all the way around the wheel.

Front spokes rarely fail, simply because their work is that much easier. Out back, the hub gears typically challenge our efforts to install any replacement spokes on the road. They'll stand right in the way; some of their number will only be removed on a bench vise. And so we instead attempt to compensate for the spoke's absence.

Our triage method is less horseshoes than hand grenades; you should loosen the brake's quick-release while you work. The spoke's resignation will have released all the tension it had been providing to the wheel, allowing those spokes just opposite to drag the rim way the hell over to their side. Short of securing a replacement, our best option for straightening the rim is to equalize the spoke tension as best might be possible, across that particular spot. Loosen the two spokes immediately opposite the broken spoke's evacuated position, to begin, all the way down to a noodle-like consistency. Depending on the results, you might also tighten the broken spoke's nearest lateral comrades. Where possible, limit your corrections to those pairs of spokes immediately adjacent to the gap. The wheel will be left with a drastic hop until you're able to fill in its gap at least.

It's better to actually replace any missing spokes if your distances are ambitious. You'll need the appropriate cassette or freewheel tool, as well as the right spoke wrench and the right spoke. The removal tools, described momentarily, are quite small; it is the requisite leverage that might weigh you down.

Almost all of the spokes enjoy fourteen-gauge threading for the nipple—as well as the characteristic elbow bend, just before the head—but their total length is measured in millimeters. Differences among hub and rim dimensions, spoke lacing patterns, and wheel sizes yield a blizzard of distinct spoke lengths. Measure any potential suitors against those spokes already populating your wheel.

Truly special touring bikes braze small bridges to one of the chainstays, upon which to stock the replacement spokes in the front, drive and neutral lengths, that might be required. You might tape your spares to a seatstay, lacking such. Realistically, the grand tourists among us will probably do best to just pack a few drive spokes. These break the soonest; their length can usually fill in for the others. Don't forget the nipples!

Improvised replacement spoke

Freewheels and cassettes look quite similar at first glance. On the road, we always hope to spy the flat lip of a distinct cassette lockring positioned atop the cogs, because they're *so* much easier to deal with. Alternately, you may be able to wind the freewheel off with a big wrench, alternately—provided it isn't rusted in place and assuming you're reasonably strong. Or you might even search out a nice farmer with a vise to loan, but the splines atop your freewheel's midsection only answer to one of more than a dozen distinct freewheel removal tools.

Park Tool's FR-1C is far and away the most common, but some of the others look quite similar. The wrong one will quite easily strip the splines from its target. Then you'll really be screwed. "Almost fits" is a recipe for destruction. *Make sure you finger-tighten the quick-release skewer or locknut atop the extraction tool to hold it in place.* Back it off as you go. Riding the bike serves to continually tighten the freewheel's grip on the hub threads; it will need a good shove, at least before it begins to loosen.

Fresh spokes will sometimes slip right over the tops of single-speed freewheels. With the larger multispeed freewheels, our only other option is replacements that are installed by alternative means, such as the bladed aero spokes that slot backward into the hub. Replacements might even be fashioned from a longer and previously beheaded spoke, given patience and a good pair of pliers, assuming the dead soldier was the longer one. A spent road spoke might be bent to fill in on a mountain wheel, for example.

Bent axles are not uncommon with the old threaded freewheel hubs because their design stuffs the drive-side bearings way back behind the freewheel. The axle's busy front porch is hardly braced at all; its roof sags quite easily. The newer freehub design supports the axle more sincerely by moving the bearings to the outside of a clutch mechanism known as the "freehub body." A gear cassette slips over the top and a lockring holds it in place. You'll need leverage from two directions at once to successfully challenge their embrace, but not nearly so much of it.

A few distinct lockrings have emerged over the years, but the great majority of cassettes coincide with Shimano's Hyperglide profile. Use Park's FR-5GC unless your axle is solid, in which case you'd want the regular old FR-5C instead. At the shop, brace the cassette with a chain whip whilst spinning the lockring free with a distinct Hyperglide tool. But the svelte

Cassette with top cog and lockring

roadside cassette tools such as the Pamir Hypercracker or the Stein Mini Cassette Lock tool are necessarily more resourceful. The bicycle chain levers against a Hyperglide tool pressed to the frame; the pedals kick in the leverage.

Flip the bike upside down and remove the wheel, as well as the quick-release skewer or locknuts, and slot your tool into the cassette lockring. Put the wheel back on the bike, making sure the Hypercracker's lip catches between the chainstays. (The Stein's toe will fit behind the seatstay for removal, or under the chainstay for reinstallation.) Turning the *pedals* backward will remove the lockring, and turning the *wheel* forward will retighten it once you're done.

Both the lockring and its cassette are faced with yet more splines, but these are small enough to merely ratchet against each

REMOVING A CASSETTE

1: Install cassette removal tool on wheel

2: Mount wheel in frame, positioning tool between stays against chainstay

3: Turn pedals backward to remove lockring

4: To reinstall, lever tool against seatstay and turn wheel forward

other to better keep the lockring's promise. This same feature also causes the cassette's tenuous compact to give quite suddenly under enough pressure. Be ready for it.

We can reuse the old spoke nipples, most of the time. You need to remove both the tire and its rim strip to replace them. Note that any nipples dropped into the deep aero-section rims probably won't make it out the other side, preferring instead to merrily rattle around the interior. You have to shake them out. It's better to introduce a surrogate: thread a spare spoke into the nipple's base to act as a launch platform, and twirl the nipple up and away as it engages the threads of the new spoke.

The spoke heads' orientation alternates on the hub flange, facing in or out. In terms of the spoke lacing, any new kids we install will learn the ropes by observing their more established peers. In the case of standard three-cross spoke lacing, a new spoke goes over two others and under a third before meeting its nipple at the rim. Don't worry about bending the spokes; the steel is resilient. Those spokes exiting to the outside of the hub flanges will actually need to bend a little more in order to reach the rim below: use your thumb to press the spoke's natural arc into place with the flattened profile of the others before bringing it up to tension.

We can use the spokes' standing committee for a reference once again when bringing the new member up to tension. Generally speaking, the nipple will make quite a few turns before establishing a useful tension. The original break will have reverberated all around their precocious circle; you'll probably need to make a few other small adjustments to get the wheel true again.

3: SEATS & SEATPOSTS

Excepting a dwindling scattering of clunky old relics, together with a few odd BMX examples, the upright bikes mount their saddles on the same sorts of platforms. Twin rails traversing the saddle's length are installed into a clamp atop the seatpost, which in turn is secured either by nuts to both sides or by a solitary bolt beneath.

In either case, none of the seat clamp's hardware should be loose. You should always do a full bolt check before any major bike trip, testing the purchase of each component with the proper tools. (You should also check in on the cranks, pedals, handlebars, stem, brakes, bearing systems, and any racks. It's not strictly poetic, but very much worth the time.)

A seat that is loose to begin with will only loosen further. It might not fall off the bike—today, at least—but crucial aspects of the seatpost clamp hardware will be rendered useless long before that point. All seat clamps face pairs of splined surfaces against each other to help determine the saddle's particular position; riding them loose simply grinds the splines down to tinfoil. You'll be left to finalize the saddle adjustment by means of the hardware's tightness alone, which, given that the threads involved are easily small enough to strip out, may become tenuous or even impossible.

So, if you do notice your seat becoming loose whilst riding, you really should stop and tighten it. Nice and snug. Almost all of the nuts we find straddling the old-fashioned straight posts should be tightened with a 14-mm box wrench; a few go for the 13-mm instead. The bolts beneath modern Laprade-style clamps answer to a 6-mm Allen key. With the far less common microadjust arrangements, first adjust the smaller bolt to set the seat's angle—using a 3- or 4-mm key, typically—before tightening the clamp with the 5-mm.

We might hope the loose saddle's dangerous wriggling is unique unto itself, but the proliferation of low-end suspension seatposts has muddled the clarity of this important signal. Worthier examples can be found, but the cheaper models—far and away the majority—will loosen with use. You'll need to stop and dismount to determine whether the saddle or its post is to blame.

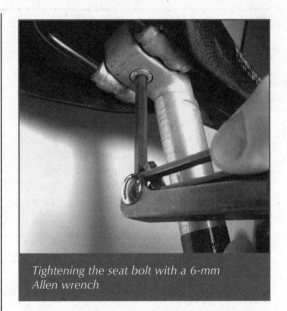

Tightening the seat bolt with a 6-mm Allen wrench

Two bolts indicate a micro-adjust style post: they'll set the seat's angle like a seesaw

Some of the cheap shock posts might be firmed up, until they fade again at least. Does a large splined ring feature beneath the shock boot? Tighten this down into the post with your hands, as far as it will go. Keep the reflex handy; it'll keep loosening until you replace the damned thing.

The chintzy, elasticized gel seat pads are about as reliable, in that there's nothing you can do to keep them from squirming around as you try to ride your bike. As with the cheaper shock posts, it's better to track down a seat you find comfortable. This question of good seating has already been run to ground many times over, leaving ragged scars across the countryside, but the controversy is reliably renewed for transient marketing purposes. Seat genres are thus given to range across a carefully defined spectrum, from performance to comfort, for men and women both. The "best" option hence remains an essentially subjective consideration, though discernible tendencies have also emerged to coincide with the range of our ambitions. Women's saddles tend to be shorter and wider; the cutaway midsections are more universal. And as might be imagined, the firmer padding will prove more durable and resilient than the salesman's discounted foam rubber cushions.

More so than its style, the saddle's position on the bike can really make or break your riding experience. The seat height is critical, down to the millimeter; our miscalculations tend toward the low end.

Novice riders commonly prefer a flat-footed purchase on Earth, when seated on the bikes, and from this perspective the conventional bicycle frames might well have been designed by taller alien beings. In fact, the saddle heights required for healthy leg extensions typically find us tiptoeing the ground when seated. The pedals also need the clearance to avoid scraping the ground on turns, of course, and so it is we're boosted to a commanding view. You might be better served with a recumbent or semirecumbent bike, if you find these arrangements untenable.

The saddle's rails allow us to pitch them back and forth atop their posts to further refine the pedaling position or our reach to the handlebars. (Handlebar positioning is more directly addressed through the stems; see Chapter 4.) And we might attribute extraterrestrial origins to some of the saddles as well, given their far-flung profiles, but they are all meant to rest as level as possible. The better yours matches our own planet's horizon line, the more comfortable you'll be.

A poor saddle position makes itself known, given the practice—your knees will start to ache. You might sort things out on your own, through trial and error, but more scientific answers will present themselves with a frame-fitting session at your local bike shop. In general terms, tension behind the knee suggests a saddle slung too low. The sublime reassurance of a good fit quietly trumps the shock posts' more saccharine charms; it's really one or the other.

The seatposts themselves should not trouble us on the road, beyond the aforementioned chintzy suspension design. The bolt(s) or quick-release lever binding the post in the frame should be made tight enough to hold the post's position. All seatposts are traced with self-explanatory maximum height lines to help preserve the frame's structural integrity; ignore them at your own risk.

If ever the quick-releases tempt you to swap seats with your buddy, you should know that they will probably need to come off their posts first. The sizes, arriving in .2-mm increments, are etched to their exteriors. The fit should be snug. The wrong post will simply slip down into the frame, if it fits at all. You might be able to convince the binder to hold a position regardless, arguing with enough torque, but such excess may only strip its threads. The effort will also compress the seat tube more than it is ever meant to be, which—with the less malleable carbon-fiber or alloy frames, at least—will eventually crack the frame.

Those among us bouncing atop the shock posts will want to keep track of any shims that might be wedged between the post and frame. The Nobel laureates distributing these gems have each greeted our forest with single seatpost sizes, meaning to stand in as lowest common denominators. The shims are often required as intermediaries. The suspension posts' central role lies in *roughly* approximating the natural resilience associated with quality steel frames, which is lost entirely on the aluminum frames; the sloppy guesswork around the sizing suggests an unfortunate unity of purpose.

You might mark the seat's optimal position with a stripe of electrical tape around its post, for transportation or storage purposes, but more generally you should not need to take it with you when you park. The seatpost's absence beckons up to the gathering clouds, daring them to fill the frame's inviting seat tube with any rain and snow that might become available…the elements will oblige. Bottom brackets are quite happy to rust in place inside their frames, given the slightest opportunity; you'll be left with something of a mechanical time bomb. Invest a few bucks in a seat leash if you're worried about theft. Better yet, replace the quick-release with a bolt or locking skewer.

Quick-release? No thanks!

4: Handlebars & Stems

The handlebars and stems join balance with momentum in ways only the road understands. We fare quite poorly in their absence.

Neither element loosens spontaneously. Each holds out for a jarring bump in the road, or a sharp yank on the grips—as when dodging obstacles, for example—before giving way to the inevitable. The vibrations absorbed with riding may erode the resolve of any bolts already slightly loose; the load-bearing fixtures up front feel these before most.

Any stem that allows its bars to become less than perpendicular to the front wheel requires immediate attention. Hop off the bike and stand in front of the handlebars, clamping the front wheel between your feet. This vantage provides for a solid reference on how well the stem is aligned, comparing against the tire below. It also leaves you well positioned to test the stem's purchase once you've tightened it.

Your bike is set up with either a quill or threadless stem, depending on its age and pedigree. Whichever the case, we'll want to conclude any adjustments made with a righteous examination: you should not be able to move the handlebars from side to side when clamping the wheel between your feet. Anything less is not safe. (Those stems featured on department store bikes incorporate weaker designs and materials and will sometimes flex a bit under such pressure. But the safest among these will return to squarely face the front.)

Most bikes on the road today use the older quill stem design, which enlists an expander bolt to brace against the interior of the fork's steerer tube. Bolt heads feature atop *nearly* all the stems, but those used with quill stems *almost* always require either a 6-mm Allen or a 13-mm box wrench. (Exceptions are quite rare, in either case.)

The expander's base will sometimes hunker down and rust in place inside the steerer tube. The bolt will simply unthread straight up; the stem won't loosen at all. Most of the time we're able to break up such sloppy embraces easily enough. Try tapping the bolt's head down with something heavy.

Mountain quill stem

The stem's relative height may also be changed. Lower elevations lend improvements in both speed and control; higher altitudes favor more relaxed riding positions. The floor level should be reasonably self-evident, but the ceiling height must yield to a pair of more subtle restrictions. Quill stems trace maximum height lines around their stalks, much as the seatposts do; it is just as foolish to ignore their emphatic suggestions. You'll want to keep an eye on the cables as well, to make sure the stem's new perspective does not stretch them taut when turning. This is rarely a problem with stock bikes, but it might come up if the bars or stem are replaced by less enlightened mechanics. Stretched cables really screw things up after a few laps.

A loose headset is pretty obvious— the steering gets hazy and the front end

Road quill stem

rattles more over bumps—but it's easy enough to stop and find out for sure. Clamp the front brake and see if you can rock the handlebars back and forth. Your headset should only spin in perfect circles, without wobbling back and forth.

The headset bearings churning beneath our quills are adjusted independently of the stems, by means of the distinctly broad and flat headset wrenches. A portable version is available in the common 32-mm size; the rest are somewhat bigger and heavier. We prefer a pair of them actually, to countertighten the headset's bearing cup against its locknut. You should overtighten both just a bit, lacking the second wrench, before backing the cup up hard against the locknut.

The more modern threadless headsets unify the bearing and stem adjustments beneath

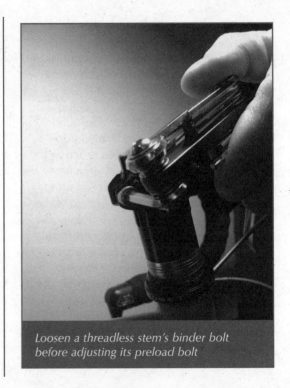

Loosen a threadless stem's binder bolt before adjusting its preload bolt

one central command. The fork's steerer tube rises up past its headset; the stem wraps around it. A preload bolt atop the stem's cap threads into a fitting inside the steerer, compressing the headset bearings to a useful adjustment; another shot through the stem's side clamps it to the steerer.

Excepting of those systems used with a handful of pretentious carbon-fiber road forks, the preload bolt is set with a 5-mm Allen key. The binder bolt(s) might ask after a 5- or 6-mm. Some of the original threadless stems hid their binders beneath small plastic plugs, which we can pry up with screwdrivers; more modern examples often line them up in pairs.

If ever your threadless headset becomes loose, you'll first want to dismount and fully loosen the stem's binder bolt(s). Counterintuitive, but very important.

The stem must be free to slide down the steerer tube in order for the preload bolt to press its headset together. *Be sure to loosen anything else bolted to the steerer tube, such as cable hangers.*

The preload itself should be tightened gradually and sparingly. Many older threadless headsets suspend their preload bolts within soft plastic caps; they sink right through easily enough.

Bounce the front end a couple of times before aligning and retightening the stem's binder bolt(s) and any cable hangers to ensure the headset bearings are fully seated. The headset should not rattle at all, though other elements might. Wrap your fingers around the lower headset cup, squeeze the front brake, and nudge the handlebars back and forth: you should not feel any lateral play between the fork and its bearing cup.

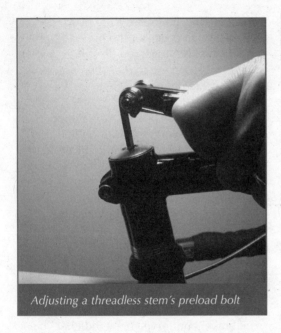

Adjusting a threadless stem's preload bolt

If your threadless stem becomes loose enough to lose its alignment, we can assume it has lost track of the headset's bearing adjustment as well. It's always best to check on both layers of the threadless sandwich whenever one or the other loosens.

On the road, the height of a threadless stem might be adjusted by one of two methods; either way, begin by removing the preload bolt and its cap. Many threadless systems incorporate spacers for just such purposes, mounted above or below the stem; it's simple enough to improve upon their sequence. Alternately, if the stem clamps the handlebars within a removable faceplate, you'll be able to invert its angle by removing and reinstalling the stem itself. A well-built bicycle provides for cables just long enough to allow for the stem's tallest possible position, but new bars and stems can erase this calculus. Make sure that none of the cables will bind at any point in the handlebars' rotation.

The faceplates are removed under the auspices of a 4-, 5-, or 6-mm Allen key. They show up with more recent quill stems, as well. As with the threadless design, it's just a much better way of doing things. With any of these, you need to make sure the faceplate ends up centered as best as possible across its two (or four) bolts.

Older quill and threadless stems wear no masks. They brace the handlebars with solitary binder bolts, the heads of which may face the rear. These should be tightened with a 5- or 6-mm Allen.

This *should* have concluded the stems' discussion, but vacuous marketing is sometimes allowed to trump proven engineering, and so it is we're given the so-called adjustable stems, which in recent years have arrived in both quill and threadless versions. Either essentially comprises an ill-conceived hinge, angling away between fork and handlebars. The thought was to provide for easy and quick stem adjustments—as if the existing arrangements were somehow complex or difficult—yet these strange new fruits have also demonstrated a prevailing tendency to loosen over time, no matter how well they might have been secured prior to departure.

The most common version shoots a single bolt through a conspicuous pivot point while an accomplice lurking beneath presses matching sets of splines together to finalize a given adjustment. This holds a position well enough, but the pivot bolt's *lateral* alignment draws in all the stress and vibrations that riding visits upon the

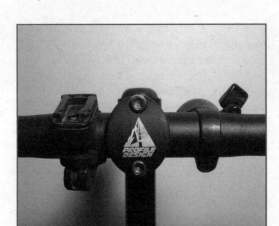
Faceplate

handlebars, the sum of which predictably overwhelms the poor bolt's reasoning. Riding the stem loose only bounces the stem's two halves against each other, widening the gaps between them and effectively making the problem permanent.

It's not difficult to replace an adjustable stem with a more useful one, given the opportunity. They're all modern enough to wear the faceplates; you merely swap the one for the other. If you do find yourself riding atop an adjustable stem, you'll want to do all you can to make sure the stem's pivot bolt stays tight. Test it before you leave, and do the same again if you even *suspect* the handlebars might be less than secure. The pivot bolt is typically faced with too-shallow sockets for a 5-mm Allen key, at either end. Only one of these will tighten, but from the outside they're identical, so you should test both. Take care to hold the wrench firmly atop its target whilst working; you'll find the curiously superficial hardware strips easily.

Brake and shift levers can loosen as well, as can the aero bars and bar-end extensions, if they weren't tightened well enough in the first place. But that's really the extent of it; you won't need to worry about the spontaneous unraveling we worry about with the adjustable stems. The agents perched atop the bars need *just enough* guidance to stand their ground. Think firm handshakes.

Much of what we clamp to the handlebars fits hardened steel bolts into aluminum fixtures, and the wrong attitude will only screw things up. The steel simply erases the softer alloy threads, given enough leverage; whatever it once was will be left to hang loose. Handlebar-mounted components of any sort should be tightened *only* until they cannot be rotated on the handlebar. (Some SRAM mountain-brake levers close up their circles before reaching this point, remaining just loose enough to roll out of the way of any serious impacts. We might also redeem the stripped bar ends and levers, sometimes, by drilling them out for larger bolts. But nobody packed a drill, right?)

The brake levers on mountain bikes are meant to ride around 45 degrees from level. Anything less will make us bend the wrists in order to brake, which can become dangerous. Those astride the city and cruiser handlebars should be mounted closer to perpendicular for similar reasons. Almost all the brake and shift levers need to be tightened with Allen wrenches; older and cheaper units may need a big screwdriver instead.

Tightening a mountain brake lever

If you positively cannot find the fastening bolt on your older mountain-style brake levers, it might subscribe to the classic road bike methodology, which has traditionally secreted the fastening bolts within the brake levers themselves. Open the brake's quick-release and squeeze the lever in order to access the bolt's head within. The oldest examples ask after the big screwdriver as well, or perhaps a smaller metric socket. The rest need 4- or 5-mm Allen keys. Your implement needs to nudge the cable out of the way to accomplish its mission; this is easier done with the Allens.

Shimano's more recent STI dual control levers relocate the (5-mm Allen head) bolt to the side of the brake lever, and Campagnolo's Ergopower levers pull off a similar trick. In either case, the bolt picks a hiding spot just beneath the edge of the lever's rubber hood, which we need to pry up for access.

Tightening a road brake lever

It's highly unusual for bars or stems to break, at this point in history. Other equally dramatic things will happen first. But you should know that the older steel handlebars can rust out from their insides, irrespective of how well their chrome plating keeps its cool retro shine. I once knew a pair to break at the stem when the bike was knocked over, actually. At the far end of the spectrum, the quite rare but recurring incidence of warranty recalls around high-end ultralight bars and stems suggests the product-testing regimen has on occasion become too public, but this only means you'll want to stay in touch with your local bike shop to learn of any warranty recalls.

5: BRAKES

The many forms of stopping power unleashed by ingenuity, enterprise, and the passage of time arrive in a broad range of styles, yet their effectiveness typically boils down to the same few points. The brakes, their pads, and the wheels must all be properly installed. The braking surfaces should also be relatively dry and clean, the pivot points lubricated, and the brake cables adjusted correctly and free to move. Your brakes will periodically require new pads, as well as the occasional more thorough servicing, yet we're often able to optimize their performance by the roadside as well.

Make sure the wheels are centered in the frame before adjusting any brake. Compare the tire's centerline against the fender and

brake holes drilled in the frame or fork above; adjust and tighten the axle's quick-release lever or locknuts accordingly.

The different braking systems are aligned with the frame and wheel by a number of distinct methods; pad-adjustment protocols vary as well. The general guidelines for brake pad and cable adjustments are outlined as follows; refer to pages 67 through 72 for details on particular braking systems.

All the rim-mounted systems afford their brake pads windows of vertical adjustment, and in every case we like the pads to become precisely parallel to the rim, centered between its upper and lower edges. The pads would happily gouge long canyons from the tires' sidewalls, lacking better guidance, through which the pent-up inner tube would earnestly try to escape. At the same time, it's no good at all if the pads dive-bomb the spokes. Note that (nonhydraulic) rim brake pads descend through small arcs before touching down to the rim's surface; their resting positions might appear to be slightly higher against the rim.

Nonhydraulic rim brake pads are often somewhat quieter and more effective if the *toe in* is set correctly, with the pad's front edge angled to touch down on the rim just *slightly* ahead of the tail. The gesture counters the minor vibrations generated through braking, to put it in a nutshell, but these jitters are much less of a concern with the shorter and weaker sorts of brakes. Older centerpull and sidepull brakes often get by without; newer dual-pivot sidepulls, cantilever, and V brakes should probably get toed in. Imagine a thin coin sandwiched under the tail when the nose hits the rim.

Nicer brakes often use cartridge brake pads, which mount removable rubber pads within more permanent aluminum carriages. Various older brakes sheathed their pads within similar boxes as well, but the cartridges are distinct in that they leave their tail gates wide open, securing their cargo by other means—a minor screw with the road pads, or a tiny retaining pin in the case of cantilever or V-brake cartridges.

The pads themselves are best installed or removed with the aid of a vise to hold the carriages, whilst the spent erasers are chiseled out with a screwdriver, and to provide a hard flat surface against which to press the new ones in. The brakes themselves lack the mass to fill in for either function, so on the road we begin by dismounting the carriages from their brake arms. Prying the old pads out is none too difficult, given a little patience, and with luck you'll find a suitable surface for pressing the new ones in. Some car's idle hood, or maybe that granite stairway over there…you get the idea.

Be sure to align the distinct left- and right-side cartridges with their prescribed lateral inclinations, with their exits facing the rear. Reinstall the pads' retaining pins or screws before riding away! This is only possible once they've been fully pressed into position.

Standardized inserts are available to fit sidepull, cantilever, and V-brake cartridge pads, but you won't be able to mix and match. They each carry the aforementioned lateral inclinations as well; the leftward pad probably will not fit in the right-side cartridge.

Newly installed cables also stretch out as their pads wear down, and so it is that brake levers commonly start to feel looser with use. They will eventually bottom out on the handlebars, left to their own devices. And then there will be no stopping you! Stop and tighten up the brake cables before you even *see* the edge of the cliff. This is easily accomplished with special pliers known as the "fourth hand," a solitary monk among tools serving few other purposes. Only the most devout mechanics take one on the road. Lacking such salvation, your best hope toward redemption arrives with the *barrel adjusters*, which intervene along the cable's path to lengthen or shorten its housing, effectively decreasing or increasing the distance a cable must travel to execute decisions.

We may find a barrel perched atop the brake itself or riding the lever's tip, but really they show up anywhere along the cable's length. We need to wind the barrel adjuster up and out of its base in order to increase the cable's tension and tighten the brakes, and vice versa. The barrel adjusters governing brake cables wear small nuts or knurled collars around their necks, which are spun all the way down to finalize a given adjustment.

Even the longest barrels run out of threads eventually. It's best to refill them before reaching that point by tightening the cable at its binder bolt. A 5-mm Allen key or a smaller metric socket does the trick. Thread the barrel's collar up as far as it'll go, twirl the barrel all the way back into its base, and pull the cable tighter beneath its binder. A short segment of the cable will have been flattened beneath the binder's steel-toed boot; use this as a reference point with any adjustments.

It's easiest to tighten up a brake cable if you're first able to momentarily release the brakes' spring tension. There are older, simpler ways to do so without relying upon the fourth hand's enlightenment. Here again, see pages 67 through 72. *Make sure to test any brake cable you adjust before riding.* Squeeze the lever as hard as you can to make sure it is well and truly secure.

In terms of their performance, the brakes function within a grand paradox. Each works best with clean and dry surfaces, but our travels easily and often depart from such nirvanic states. The debris flung up by road and trail angrily grinds away between the pads and their braking surfaces whenever we try to slow things down, methodically wearing away at both. There opens a

Pandora's box of loose, loud, and less-effective brakes, against which we set the course of our mechanical energies.

Brakes in active use may require new pads annually, but the rims' sidewalls tend to last a few years. Disc brake rotors are almost immortal, though their pads are not. Note that rim-mounted brake pads are marked with maximum wear lines, which you ignore at your own risk. The pads' steel bases will carve up the rim past these boundaries, and things will go south in a hurry.

Brakes have evolved considerably over the years—from flint axes to simple muskets to full-on artillery pieces—such that it is now possible to stop with far more force than we ever actually need. Is this a great time or what? First to offer any resistance was the veteran sidepull brake, an inverted smile mounted directly above the tire,

so named for its off-center control cable. Sidepulls are found on most road bikes, as well as various ancient mountain and city bikes. The delicate and aquiline originals have long since given way to shorter and more rigid successors, yielding meaningful improvements in performance.

The sidepull's binder bolt clamps to the lateral end of one brake arm, and the quick-release—a small switch flipped up and down with the fingers—usually mounts upon the other. Some sidepulls move the quick-release upstairs instead, strapping a stout rod across the lever's snout that we slide aside to release the brakes. Yet others, from Shimano, mount a boxy spring-loaded button to the side of the lever. The sidepull's quick-release might lend the discretion to ride home on wheels less than true, *so long* as its brake lever is not able to bottom out on the handlebar.

Older road caliper brake

Pad adjustments are very much point and shoot with the sidepulls. The pads' fixing bolts charge straight out of vertical windows on the brake arms, to be capped with nuts and washers. Line up your 5-mm Allen or 10-mm socket wrench atop its target, hold the pad where you want it to be, and make it so.

Many recent sidepull pads incorporate pairs of squat concave and convex washers, which allow for a toe in. V-brake pads yield a similar advantage, given the judicious arrangement of their washer sets. These usually work with the sidepulls in a pinch, though some narrower road-bike forks balk at the V pads' extended tails. In either case, it's easy enough to hold the pads at slight angles to the rim as you tighten them down.

If the wheel is both centered and true, yet a brake pad still rides too close to its rim, you'll want to verify the alignment of the brake itself. The oldest sidepulls dedicated no special hardware to such purposes; we center them manually. Loosening the nut anchoring the brake to frame or fork allows one to reposition the caliper as needed, but given the tools it's quicker to grip both the anchoring nut and the brake's nose cone—using a pair of 10-mm sockets or wrenches, typically—and gradually turn them simultaneously. That anchor nut needs to end up really tight, either way.

Older sidepulls are topped with pairs of nuts, which are meant to be countertightened against each other, yet their accord should not be *so* tight as to hinder the brake arms' movements beneath. Ideally, the sidepull's adjustment should allow it *just* enough clearance to open and close, without any lateral play along its axis.

Back at the shop, we use one of several ultra-thin brake wrenches to cement any new deals between the top nut and its slimmer subordinate, none of which we expect to find in a roadside repair kit. If your sad old caliper does loosen on the road, you can temporarily replace both nuts with a single 6-mm nylock nut, found at the nearest hardware store…or perhaps on that abandoned bike carcass you passed a ways back. Don't be afraid to scavenge.

More recent sidepulls are professionally centered with wrench flats cut to the sides of the spring's mounting block, meant for the aforementioned brake wrenches. But in the field we use one of the manual centering methods described previously. You may need to pop a cosmetic rubber stopper out of the nose cone with some of these nicer middle-aged sidepulls, before inserting an Allen wrench therein.

You'll need to refill the brake's barrel adjuster, following with successive corrections to its cable tension, and this will be easiest if you first suspend your sidepull's spring tension. Remove the wheel and squeeze the brake pads together; this should create enough slack to simply tug the cable tighter at the binder bolt. If you're not able to take the wheel off, it's usually possible to pinch the brake spring out of the way instead, by prying one end free with a small screwdriver.

The dual-pivot sidepulls are found on most contemporary road bikes. They take a tip from the cantilevers and the V brakes, splitting their pivot between points to either side of the wheel, optimizing the braking leverage available through the same old mounting hole. Their amplified power is well served by the modern road brake pads' toe-in capacities, but we're able to

Dual-pivot caliper brake

substitute traditional road or even V-brake pads as needed.

The dual-pivot is centered by means of a small screw set into its shoulder, adjusted with either a screwdriver or a 2-mm Allen key. The screw is under tension and typically turns only grudgingly; bear down hard on the screwdriver to avoid stripping its target. The average dual-pivot gets by with a single screw, but some from Campagnolo use two. That farthest from the cable centers the brake; its partner governs the spring tension. A further minority from Tektro complement the old-school brake wrench flats with solitary 2-mm Allen screws, which seem most concerned with the spring tension.

As with the original sidepulls, it's best to remove the wheel and clasp the brake pads together before tightening the cable at its binder bolt. It's probably your only other option, absent the fourth hand. The typical dual-pivot spring is shorter and stronger than that which we find with a traditional sidepull; you'll have a hell of a time popping it out, let alone back in.

The centerpull brakes were popular among road bikes before the dual-pivots were even a gleam in their inventors' eyes, and they were also the first to use counterbalanced pivots. Their development was less sophisticated in other respects. The prevailing design flexes too much, absorbing a portion of the force assigned to the brake lever; it does not stop you nearly as quickly as the dual-pivot does. Nor will the stoic centerpull provide any centering hardware; you'll need to loosen the brake's 10-mm anchor nut to straighten things out. It's quicker to align your centerpull by tapping the shoulder spring on the wayward side with a hammer and punch, given the tools, but the anchor always needs to end up nice and snug.

The classic centerpull deployment joins the quick-release with a barrel adjuster, installing their ensemble just below the stem or seatpost. Take full advantage of the barrel; you'll need two wrenches and a few minutes to tighten up the centerpull's cable hanger. First release the short straddle cable strung across the hanger's lap, either with the quick-release or by removing the wheel, clutching the brake pads together and pivoting one end of the straddle out of the slot topping either brake arm. The hanger's binder bolt can be challenging to tighten, given its unsupported position; use two wrenches and test it thoroughly.

Most centerpulls favor the sidepull brake pads, and these at least can also work with the V-brake pads, but some will insist on the cantilever pads' smooth posts instead. The cantilever brakes enjoy a long and splendid history, stretching from the earliest mountain and touring rigs to current cyclo-cross bikes, which is to say adjustability and sophistication vary a great deal. The essential design delivers tangible improvements; even the ancients should stop you sooner than sidepulls or centerpulls.

Those frames and forks willing to consider the cantilevers erect brake bosses in set positions to either side of the wheel, upon which the twin brake arms pivot, floating on thin films of grease. A healthy and ambitious cantilever brake balances its pads a millimeter or two to either side of the wheel, but cables stretch, rubber wears, and eventually the rust creeps in. With time, the springs fight to keep their house in order. A pad may even start dragging

Cantilever brake

ass on the rim, slowing our progress with a passive but meaningful ambivalence.

On the road, we motivate such slackers by refocusing the centering apparatus or cranking up the tension, depending on the details. In either case, we want to conclude any adjustments made by thoroughly wiggling the brake arms back and forth across their bosses, such that our corrections really sink in. Finally, something that involves wiggling!

Unless you're merely twiddling a centering screw, described momentarily, it's best to open the cantilever's quick-release before adjusting either its centering or spring tension. Cantilever straddle cables arrive in a few distinct styles, but the quick-release always opens the same way. One end of the straddle ends in a fat metal button, which slips into position through a slot on the brake arm, given a little slack. Think of it as a primitive combination lock; line up the cable under the gap and slide it on out.

Nearly all cantilevers derive their energies from coiled springs, leveraged between each brake arm and points on either the base of the brake boss or an adjustable nut. This last governs both the brake's centering and spring tension; it may appear on one or both sides.

Your mobile kit likely doesn't include the particular wrench you need to turn such a nut—sizes again vary—but you shouldn't really need it. Loosen the brake arm's mounting bolt, using a 5- or 6-mm Allen key, or perhaps a 10-mm socket. The nut will simply move with the brake arm, once loosened, unless it's rusted in place. Reposition the package as needed—inclined slightly more toward the horizon to increase the tension—and hold it right

there until the arm's mounting bolt makes it all the way back home. You may have to do this a few times before landing on the best answer. Don't forget to wiggle.

If the nut only shows up on one brake arm, you can complement any adjustments made by removing the opposite brake arm and repositioning its spring, the tail end of which normally burrows into a small hole at the base of the brake boss. It's *usually* given a choice of three options, arranged vertically; kicking the spring up a notch increases its tension dramatically.

This horseplay with the nuts and springs usually takes a few minutes, so many cantilevers opt for a centering screw instead, installed near the base of one brake arm. Tightening will increase the spring tension on the screw's side, moving its brake arm away from the rim, and vice versa. The corrections are meant to echo across the straddle cable, influencing the opposite brake arm's position as well. Use a screwdriver or a 2-mm Allen, depending.

The oldest cantilevers were foolhardy pioneers, galloping into the void bereft of any particular centering paraphernalia. We can cajole them toward a centered effect by jacking their tired springs up a hole on the brake bosses on one or both sides, or by offsetting the pads' positions on the brake arms. You can even convince the cable hanger to favor one side or the other by bending new kinks into its straddle cable, though you'll probably need pliers to do this.

However it is you accomplish the mission, it's best to center the brakes before adjusting the pads. For all their celebrated refinement, the modern cantilevers embrace their brake pads the same way their ancestors did. The pad's long smooth post skewers the head of a squat banjo-like bolt, the tail of which darts through a pair of contoured washers framing a tall window in the brake arm, before emerging to submit beneath a sturdy nut.

The curious hardware collection provides the best approach to toeing in the brake pads when first the cantilevers were born—an improvement that first became relevant with their enhanced stopping power—but the assembly breaks down easily enough. Grip the pad's mounting bolt with one wrench whilst turning its nut with another to tighten or release an errant brake pad. Use a 5- or 6-mm Allen and a 10-mm box wrench, or perhaps a pair of the 10-mm.

A poorly aligned pad can simply be installed in a better position—hold it firmly in place while tightening the nut all the way down—but those erased down to their maximum-wear lines should definitely get replaced. You'll also want to make sure the cantilever's straddle cable hangs a useful distance above the brake arms, as described momentarily, before committing to any pad adjustments. Note that the upper of the two contoured washers may attempt an escape, absent the brake pad's intervention; you won't be able to get by without it.

It may be as simple as that, but many recent cantilevers are afflicted with the accursed automatic toe-in feature, a truly bad idea that torpedoes any pad adjustments you may pursue. It's simply useless fiction pushed by shady advertising hacks. If you're having trouble setting the pads up, take the mounting hardware apart and see if you can find anything resembling a spring buried therein. It may be only a

washer with a spring-loaded cut; it may even hide inside the brake arm's window. Whichever the case, dig it out and throw it the hell away. It's best to do the same for each brake arm in turn, given the time, using the others to guide your reassembly.

You'll get a better sense of how much to tighten the cable once you've centered the cantilever and set up its pads. The brake lever shouldn't bottom out on the handlebar; the pads shouldn't ride the rim. The cantilever-equipped cyclo-cross and touring bikes mount their barrel adjusters either at the cable stops or along the cables themselves, but it's more common to find a cantilever's barrel sprouting directly from its lever's snout. The brake's collected spring tension is largely suspended when we open its quick-release, allowing us to refill the barrel as needed by tugging the cable tighter beneath the binder bolt.

Most straddle cables are simple creatures, hooking up with the quick-release on one side while shooting the brake cable through a straw to the other, but we also see straddle wires hanging from distinct cable hangers. In either case, the straddle should split for the brake arms just above the frame or fork's fender hole. Anything more or less tends to compromise braking performance.

Excepting the oldest cantilevers and their newer retro imitators, which adapt lower profiles, the angles formed between the straddle and the *upper* inside edges of the brake arms should sketch a nice baseball diamond, cornering around 90 degrees all the way around. The pads may or may not want to play ball—they may have worn down or perhaps weren't set up right in the first place. Yet if your journey remains ambitious, it's worth your time to sort things out.

The cantis are still popular with cross and tour bikes, for reasons we'll examine, but everyone else has long since moved on to the linear pull brakes, which are more commonly known as V brakes. The V's twin pillars shrewdly appropriate the old cantilevers' prized bosses, rising to meet a cable shot straight over the top of the tire, optimizing the available leverage by minimizing opportunities for flex. They are the blazingly efficient technocrats amongst their peers. You will stop quickly.

The V brakes' springs burrow into holes astride the brake bosses just as the cantilevers do, but in their case the prescient centering screws hold court on either side. Turning one in increases the tension, backing its brake arm away from the rim, and the reverse is also true. The cable translates one side's adjustments to the arm opposite, helping its pair strike

V brake

a balance. As with the cantilevers, the V brakes should be centered in relation to both the wheel and its fork or frame. Here again, we facilitate their accord by wiggling the brakes across their bosses after making any adjustments.

The V's long springs usually ride right up the sides of the brake arms. In the odd event the centering screws aren't able to call their match, you might simply unclip the springs and bend in a little more tension. Don't go crazy with it, just bear down with the thumbs for a second. This should make a big difference; only the most recalcitrant of problems persists through such efforts. The brake bosses may be rusted to hell, to take one famous example, but unless you packed some emery cloth and bearing grease, they'll be staying that way for the duration.

Barring simpler redemption, our final option toward centering or reenergizing the V brakes is to remove the bolts securing them to frame or fork and jack their springs up a hole on the brake bosses, most of which provide a choice of three vertical options for the springs. The 5-mm Allen will release the arms. Moving their springs up a notch presents a cataclysmic upheaval, given the angles involved; you'll probably need to back the screws almost all the way out to get things working again.

Pad adjustments come easier once the brakes are centered. The V-brake pad's long threaded post is equipped with two pairs of concave and convex washers, one shorter and the other taller, meant to face each other across the brake arm's window. The convex washers may resemble a skewered pea, but for the pane, splitting them in twain; the concave washers become bowls for their soup.

Working in teams, the washers provide the brake pads all the flexibility required to trace the rim's profile and establish a toe-in. Their sequence is key; we'd get nothing but right angles without it. The stout nut atop their stack answers to a 5-mm Allen wrench, or possibly a 10-mm socket; simply hold the pad in place whilst tightening it down.

Your V brakes are most effective when their arms approach parallel positions, and the washers help here as well by providing a choice of options when installing brake pads. We *usually* mount the thinner pairs closest to the rim, but really it's up to the details. Mountain bikes favor ever-wider frame and fork clearances to better fit even fatter tires; it might make sense to lead with the thick washers instead. Loosened brakes are better resolved with cable adjustments; the washer positioning is more about setting up the goal posts.

The V brake's cable slopes down from one side to dive through a curved metal straw known as the "brake noodle," the tip of which slots into a hinged alleyway atop the nearest brake arm. The cable itself shoots through an accordion-like rubber boot before submitting beneath a binder bolt on the far side. The boots mean to catch debris flung up from the trails, but in practice they complicate our adjustments with the binder bolts. As with the knobbies themselves, they're usually more of a fashion accessory.

We'll need to slide the boot away from the noodle, before opening the V brake's quick-release: grasp the noodle with one hand while bracing its alleyway with the other, and pull the tip back out of its perch.

In the event you find yourself replacing parts on tour, you should know the V-brake levers pull twice as much cable as any others. Yet the mountain bike-oriented Vs have not made many friends amongst the road bikes' more doctrinaire control levers, and thus do cross and tour bikes run the old cantilever brakes. V levers may do fine atop any other cable-driven braking system, to put it in a nutshell, but they are the only ones that command the V brakes themselves.

Disc brakes are found in both cable-driven and hydraulic formats. Their stopping powers can be called remarkable and fully ridiculous, respectively. In either case, all the mounting bolts need is to be nice and

Adjusting V Brakes

1: Confirm wheel centering, adjusting as necessary

2: Confirm brake centering, adjusting as necessary

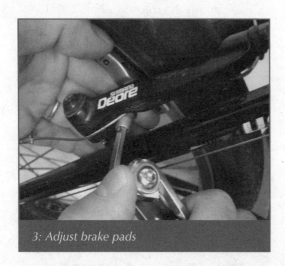

3: Adjust brake pads

4: Adjust brake cable

tight: your 5-mm Allen will suffice for the disc levers and calipers, but you'll need a T25 torx wrench to secure the rotors. (The more useful multitool kits will include this one.) The disc brakes' intrepid design is far less troubled by vibration-induced sound effects, but any kind of oil will make them scream like the audience at a horror show. We can calm things down with a clean rag and some rubbing alcohol, given the opportunity, but it's better to avoid touching the rotors altogether. Even fingerprints can set off alarms.

The brake lever's bite loosens as its pads wear down, and in time you'll need to tighten things up. The inboard pad rests in a fixed position, which is set with a large dial facing the spokes—a broad flat bolt head turned with the 5-mm Allen, or perhaps a fat quarter spun with the fingertips—while its mate grinds the rotor to a halt. First, park the fixed pad *just* loose enough to avoid dragging on the rotor before setting the outboard pad's position with the cable's barrel adjuster. Work in small increments in either case, spinning the wheel to check your work. Go for a business card's width between pads and rotor.

This textbook example might confront a few special problems. The brake pads will drag if their wheel is not *precisely* aligned with the brake calipers, for starters, and the wheel's mounting hardware needs to be nice and tight. This last may not be as simple as it sounds, unfortunately, because the standard mounting system used to fit disc calipers to bicycle forks has recently been associated with an unanticipated side effect: the design misdirects some of the energy spent with braking, such that conventional hub skewers may eventually work themselves loose. No joke. Through-axle systems such as the Tullio are immune to this problem, but pending broader renovations you'll want to keep an eye on any other fork-mounted disc brakes in your care. If ever one begins to rub, check on the wheel's mounting hardware before anything else.

A bent rotor can manifest a similar effect, assuming its wheel still spins at all—you'd need a hell of an impact to so disturb its meditation—but assuming the wheel skewer is tight, rubbing brakes will more likely trace back to a misaligned caliper. Warped rotors may only be redeemed with high science up at the bike shop, yet the wayward caliper is brought to heel easily enough. We first need to loosen both of its mounting bolts—those presiding over elongated adjustment windows—such that the caliper can scoot around at leisure. This done, tighten both brake pads as far possible: it is here, with the rotor clenched firmly between its teeth, that the caliper will most truly align with its target. Snug the caliper's mounting bolts back down right there, before easing the pads out to more critical distances.

Distance-minded tourists will want to pack spare pads for their particular disc brakes. None are much to carry, but it's not likely we'll find any in a hurry. Spent pads are simply pulled out by their tabs; replacements should click into place just as easily. Be extra gentle with the springs framing the pads, as they bend easily enough. Note that the left and right sides are distinct, and don't even try to install the wrong pads.

Both the BMX U brakes and the ancient roller-cam rigs blend ideas from centerpull and cantilever brakes. The distinct *roller* brakes snare hub-mounted lids within unyielding wire hoops, dragging their wheels to a halt. All three systems submit to lever-mounted barrel adjusters, and each also subscribes to the usual rules: their bolts should all be tight, the braking surfaces should be as clean and dry as possible, and only the pivot points should be lubricated.

Much the same is true again with the coaster brakes, which fasten their levers directly to the frame itself. We simply backpedal to stop; we only need to be sure the bolt securing lever to frame is fully tight. The tandem's drum brakes link the same reliable no-brainer technology to hand levers; we tune them as needed with the cable's barrel adjusters.

Lacking a hand brake, the fixed gear modulates speed with cog and chain alone. Both need to be quite secure, as does the rest of their kit. The fix does not work nearly as well with any play in the wheel or the cranks; its chain should be about as tight as possible. Yet the tug-of-war between stop and go loosens the chain, muddling the clarity of our most emphatic suggestions.

We tighten a fixed gear's chain by walking its wheel back in the frame's dropouts. Loosen the drive-side axle nut, squeeze the front of the wheel toward the drive-side chainstay, and hold it there whilst retightening the nut: the drive-side end of the axle creeps back in its dropout while the wheel's alignment drifts away from the frame's centerline. Loosen the neutral-side axle nut and move that end of the axle back by the same measure, tightening the nut once the wheel is centered in the frame. Repeat the sequence until the chain gives less than an inch of play when pressed. Your adjustments will hold more reliably with the aid of a BMX-style chain tensioner, mounted on the drive side.

6: DRIVETRAINS

The best way to keep a drivetrain going is simply to take care of it. On the road, the very first thing to learn is an aversion to force. Shift down to a more comfortable gear *before* climbing a hill, in other words. Precious few shifters and derailleurs are built to last; after a point, there's just no arguing with any of them. We stop pedaling when shifting internally geared hubs, but derailleur-equipped bikes shift best with just enough pressure to keep the pedals turning.

The cogs, chain, and chainrings are typically more resilient than any of their ever more complex supervisors, but the days are long and each wears with use. A cogset may service two or three chains, assuming they're replaced every 3,000 miles or so; the bigger chainrings last about as long. Keep an eye on the smaller rings; those approaching carved-out shark tooth profiles are ready to bite something else.

A toasted chain will skip around under pressure, grasping for the tired old cogs it knows so well, but skipping chains more often trace back to far simpler problems. You'll definitely want to conduct a thorough bolt check and test both derailleur and cable adjustments before writing off any drivetrain parts.

First test those fixtures securing cranks and pedals, shifters and derailleurs, cables and wheel. It sounds like math class, I know, but this alone may fix the problem.

Cinching down the crank and chainring bolts will silence many an annoying creak, for example. Test the pedal cage screws as well. Older cranks often hide their mounting bolts (or nuts) beneath dustcaps meant to guard their crucial extraction threads. Some dustcaps unscrew from these very features; the rest pry loose with a screwdriver. The crank bolts themselves answer to a 14- or 15-mm socket.

Modern cranks use broad-faced Allen bolts instead; usually 8-mm. You'll probably need the unique but very portable crank backer tool to tighten any loose chainring bolts, and possibly to unscrew various older dustcaps as well; serious tourists will want to pack one. Cogs need a little play against the wheel in order to coast, but loose cassettes can manifest very similar effects: snug down the cassette's lockring, as described on page 40, if ever you're unsure of its purchase. Your smaller Allen keys and metric sockets will suffice for testing the rest of your drivetrain components; everything should be nice and tight.

Confirm that the derailleurs are mounted correctly before investigating their adjustments. The frame's rear derailleur hanger tends to bend inward when crashed: viewed from the rear, both derailleur pulleys should line up parallel to the cogs above. The alignment is crucial; it presupposes everything else. Bent hangers are best straightened with shop tools, but it's often possible to lever them back to workable angles with a loose 5-mm Allen key. Skewer the derailleur's mounting bolt with the tool's short end; apply gradual pressure to its length. Do take your time; forceful shoves can snap the aluminum hangers.

On-the-road derailleur alignment

Front derailleurs enjoy more secure positions, but their installation takes more finesse. Their cage profiles vary—most exhibit a carefully stepped topography to favor narrower or wider gearing ranges—but the outer plate's longest plane should always rest parallel with the chainrings, and the cage itself should clear the big ring by 2 mm when shifted. We can correct either measure by repositioning the derailleur itself, which is most often secured with a single mounting bolt. You may need to release the shift cable in order to move it up or down the seat tube. Note as well that some older chainrings were born as ovals; you'll need the same clearance over their highest points.

Its alignment verified, the derailleurs' limit screws get our conideration next. But really, there's rarely anything to think about. The limit screws merely outline the range of motion; they're meant to be set when first the derailleurs are installed. None are inclined to rattle loose; further adjustments only undermine the original guesswork. The aforementioned wear and alignment issues are far more likely to cause shifting troubles, as are the cable-tension details, described momentarily.

The limit screws always feature in pairs, marked L and H, for low and high, and together they afford the chain *just* enough freedom to engage the full range of gears without hindrance. We only question their judgment when the chain is kept from a particular cog or chainring, or when it's tossed over the edge. In every case, the limit screws are dialed in to limit the derailleurs' realm, or out to increase it. Move in minor increments, checking your work with a test ride at every turn.

If the chain fails to reach the smallest cog in back, or trips over its edge entirely, you'll need to speak with the rear derailleur's high-limit (H-limit) screw. If the chain stops short of the largest rear cog—or launches into the spokes—you adjust the low-limit (L-limit) screw. Note that you may need to release the shift cable before loosening the rear derailleur's H-limit screw, lest the cable's tension nullify further adjustments on the high side. (The dumbed-down Shimano rapid-rise/low-normal derailleurs reverse the polarity of this equation by setting the low position as the derailleur's resting point; you'll eventually need to release the cable to continue loosening the L-limit screw.)

Modern rear derailleurs incorporate a further agent, known as the B-tension screw, set laterally into one of the major pivots. It is but a minor character, serving only to modulate the distance between cogs and derailleur pulleys. We need to dial the B all the way in to prevent the two from noisily riding against each other, and really that's all we may ask it to do.

Only the most disturbed front derailleurs keep the chain from one of its rings. Those merely troubled are content to scrape on the chain as we pedal. But here again, look for simpler explanations before dragging the limit screws into it. Poor derailleur positioning will sooner toss the chain, or cause it to rub in the smallest ring, while inadequate cable tension is most inclined to cause problems up top. It'll likely take a few test rides to arrive upon a good balance, once the screws are in play.

The L-limit screw chaperones the smallest chainring up front, while its partner up high watches over the big ring. We dial either in to prevent the chain from leaping free, much as we do out back, but differences among derailleur-cage profiles and gearing ranges render the low adjustment more subjective. Err on the side of caution; don't loosen the L-limit screw any more than shifting might require.

New derailleur cables stretch just as their housing seats itself further into the frame's cable stops, and eventually you'll need to tighten things up. The barrel adjusters' sheer ubiquity hints at the cable tension's influence amongst current mechanical demons: it lays a broad foundation for the tragic pantheon of shifting problems.

The old friction levers are almost ambivalent about their cable tension—they only need cables tight enough to lurch the chain to the final cog or chainring—but the indexing shift levers are positively neurotic about it. It sets the starting point for their careful ratcheting, echoing either the correct measure or the same basic misunderstanding across the full range of gears. The simple accumulation of slack can throw the whole thing off, in other words, but by the same token we only need to tune that very first *quack* to line the ducks in a row.

We're usually able to sort things out with the barrel adjusters, found atop the shift lever or the derailleur, or at points along the cable itself. We thread them out to increase cable tension, or back in to reduce it. Think gradual.

The barrel runs empty, one fine day, leaving you to refill it. First, shift the derailleur down to its resting position—where the cable is most slack—before rolling the barrel all the way back into the derailleur's basement. The cable's binder bolt typically releases beneath a 5-mm Allen key, or

ADJUSTING A REAR DERAILLEUR

1: Confirm derailleur hanger alignment

2: Test high-limit screw

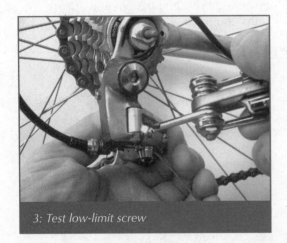

3: Test low-limit screw

4: Adjust the cable tension

perhaps a 9-mm socket; you simply pull the cable taught and clamp the binder closed again. This in itself can only provide for the roughest estimate; you need to refine it with the refreshed barrel adjuster.

Beginning from its starting point, a well-adjusted indexing shift lever carries the rear derailleur precisely one gear on its very first click. You'll likely need to push the lever slightly past this point to accomplish the shift; our measurement is taken once you let go. Viewed from behind, the rear derailleur's pulleys should line up directly beneath this second cog. Gradually turn the barrel out if the chain isn't making this jump, or back in once it begins to rasp against the following cog.

The indexing fronts are often more particular than their rearward compatriots. Some are easygoing, like the friction levers—those Campagnolo and SRAM units equipped with a range of minor clicks are merely shifted to better positions whenever the derailleur's cage rides against the chain—but most assign individual clicks to each chainring. In political terms, this makes them rigidly dogmatic. Upon confirming the derailleur's positioning and limit screws, you're left to test and adjust its cable tension until at last it makes an odd sense. Dialing the barrel out moves the derailleur cage toward the big ring, and the reverse is also true. More recent Shimano STI levers are somewhat easier to negotiate with—they award each chainring a pair of indexed positions—yet the originals will surely test the patience.

The forward-indexing ideology is further distinct to double- and triple-chainring cranksets. The triple sect is best evaluated with the chain in the middle ring, from which it should be able to hit all or at least *most* of the rear gearing range without grinding on the derailleur cage. Older seven-speed systems generally provide their chains full and clear access from this middling position; modern eight- and nine-speed setups run the chain against its patient minder at either or both extremes.

Cross-geared combinations—from the big ring to the two biggest cogs, or from the small ring to the two smallest cogs—are not good for the drivetrain parts, and the idealistic double-ring indexed front derailleurs strive to warn us of the fact by grinding on the chain in such positions. The correct cable tension only yields an indexed double-clear access to the gears we're actually *meant* to use, in other words. There's no good way around this point; you'll either adopt a measure of discretion whence shifting, or you'll scrape on by like a hack.

The chains themselves are reasonably intuitive. Those caked with rust squeak incessantly: they also shift poorly, expire far sooner, and suggest more systemic problems. Apply a bicycle-specific chain wax or gel-based lubricant before saddling up.

Chains bend quite rarely—you'd really need to jam on the levers—but most can be straightened, given a couple pairs of pliers. Identify the link(s) to straighten; attack from both sides at once.

Tight chain links are somewhat more common. Spin the pedals backward, watching the chain as it passes through the derailleur pulleys. Anything jump out at you? Test suspicious links with your fingers. Impress your suspect into the chain tool's *upper* position and give its handle a quarter turn to spread the chain plates a hair farther apart.

Adjusting a Front Derailleur

1: Confirm front derailleur's lateral orientation

2: Test front derailleur's horizontal position

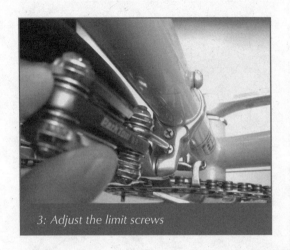

3: Adjust the limit screws

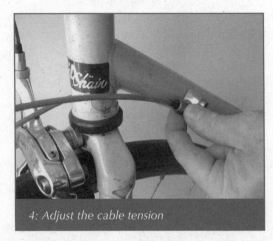

4: Adjust the cable tension

Chains are tricky. Take your time. Each link needs to be *only* loose enough to allow freedom of motion. The pins mean to extend evenly from each side—as far as this might be possible, anyway—and you really don't want to upset their apple cart. Those chains that do break under pressure will generally trace back to this very point; the adjustment really needs to be spot-on. This is why manufacturers increasingly favor master links; they eliminate all the guesswork.

Lacking such, we join a chain in the tool's *lower* saddle. The upper is only strong enough to loosen tight links; get the chain pin nice and even downstairs first.

Remove any damaged links! This will leave the chain slightly too short: unless you packed spare links for your particular chain, you'll need to dial in the rear

SRAM master link

derailleur's L-limit screw enough to compensate by closing off access to the largest cog or two. Only as such will the chain avoid stretching itself to pieces.

A worn chain will continue skipping out of gear after the cable and derailleur adjustments are verified. The cogs will also be toast, by that point, and we might wonder about a chainring or two as well. Shop tools can provide a more precise appraisal, but the truest estimation incorporates the test ride as well. Fixed gears, single-speeds, and the old three-speeds can milk old chains much longer—they have nowhere to skip off to, lacking the derailleurs' interventions—but theirs, too, will perish.

Poorly adjusted front derailleurs will sometimes allow the chain to fall off, but the same occasionally happens with perfectly healthy bikes as well. Dropping the chain isn't necessarily a big deal in itself, in other words, but you'll want to check things out if it happens twice. Flipping it back into place may become a minor pain in the ass; truly ugly examples can be lifted up with a twig. Chains are sturdy as hell, compared to certain other parts; don't be afraid to wiggle or yank them free.

Single-speed and three-speed chains should always be reasonably taut; don't let them sag. You need to lose a chain link if the dropouts prevent this. The fixed chain should be about as tight as possible—see page 87—but all the others need a little more breathing room.

The aforementioned suggestions address most drivetrain issues, but the days are long and some more interesting bikes might favor bigger problems. Rusty cables can trump our best efforts toward amelioration, as can damaged cable housing. Derailleur cages can be bent beyond use, given enough force on the shift levers. Their pivots also wear out, leaving the cage to drift back and forth across the various gears: the cheaper, the sooner. And the old chestnut of compatibility may also be dropped if less-enlightened persons have installed parts to your drivetrain. Not all parts are meant to work together, basically. Happy coincidences are unlikely amongst our beloved component manufacturers; self-indulgent territorial pissing is more the norm.

Loose cranks or pedals can easily end the ride if left unchecked. *Test them before your big trip.* Pedal threads are sturdier than others, but riding loose pedals will quickly erase them; eventually they'll simply fall off. Note that the neutral side pedal is reverse-threaded.

As a rule, the crank bolts should be about as tight as you can make them. They're press-fit to the bottom bracket axle; riding them loose widens out their fittings. The process is cumulative rather then reversible; loosened cranks will only become looser.

For practical purposes, imagine demons slumbering in the bottom bracket: riding it loose awakens them. The longer this continues, the angrier they become, eventually pulverizing the bearings and grease into silvery paste. This in itself may not stop the ride, but it will surely summon other menaces. As with any other beast, bikes will only take so much.

References

63xc.com
www.63xc.com

A website for anyone interested in taking fixed-gear bikes off-road.

A to B Magazine
www.atob.org.uk

Incorporating folding bikes, electric bikes, trailers, trikes, trains, and alternative transport into one magazine.

Adventure Cycling Association
www.adv-cycling.org

A membership organization offering the finest cycle-touring guides available. For thirty years, the National Bicycle Route Network has produced maps outlining quiet and scenic routes across North America.

Bicycle Inter-Community Action & Salvage
www.bicas.org

A cooperatively run nonprofit community center promoting education, art, and a healthy environment through bicycle advocacy and recycling.

BICYCLE ORGANIZATION ORGANIZATION PROJECT
www.bikecollectives.org/downloads/boop.pdf

A directory of do-it-yourself bike shops and community bike projects in North America.

BICYCLING EMPOWERMENT NETWORK
www.benbikes.org.za

A South African organization dedicated to poverty alleviation through the promotion of the use of the bicycle in all its forms in order to both enhance low-cost, non-motorized transport and improve public health by linking exercise to mobility.

BIKES NOT BOMBS
www.bikesnotbombs.org

Bikes Not Bombs (BNB) promotes bicycle technology as a concrete alternative to war and environmental destruction. For twenty-three years, BNB has been a nexus of bike recycling and community empowerment both in lower income neighborhoods of Boston and in the nations of the global south. BNB's programs involve young people and adults in mutually respectful leadership development and environmental stewardship, while recycling thousands of bicycles.

CAR BUSTERS
www.carbusters.org

A publication of the World Carfree Network based in Prague, Czech Republic. It serves as both an information source and a call to action, providing a full range of content from direct-action skills to the latest research developments.

CARS-R-COFFINS
www.carsrcoffins.com

One of the more credible icons of bike culture.

THE CENTRE FOR SUSTAINABLE TRANSPORTATIONS
cst.uwinnipeg.ca

An advocacy organization dedicated to achieving sustainable transportation in Canada.

CRITICAL-MASS.INFO
www.critical-mass.info

The site provides contact information in several languages for Critical Mass rides on six continents.

CYCLING & YOUR CHILD
www.personal.dundee.ac.uk/~pjclinch/
cyclingchild.htm

An online resource for parents wishing to help their children begin safe cycling.

FIXED-GEAR GALLERY
www.fixedgeargallery.com

Where fixed gears go to see and be seen.

ICE BIKE
www.icebike.org

A website providing useful information for those interested in cycling for transportation, recreation, or competition in the winter.

INTERNATIONAL FEDERATION OF BIKE MESSENGER ASSOCIATIONS
www.messengers.org

An organization dedicated to fostering a spirit of cooperation and community amongst bicycle messengers worldwide, promoting the use of pedal power for commercial purposes and ensuring the successful realization of an annual Cycle Messenger World Championships.

INTERNATIONAL HUMAN POWERED VEHICLE ASSOCIATION
www.ihpva.org

An association of national associations and organizations dedicated to promoting improvement, innovation, and creativity in the use of human power, especially in the design and development of human-powered vehicles.

MOMENTUM MAGAZINE
www.momentumplanet.com

A bimonthly publication reflecting the lives of people who ride bikes. The magazine also provides the inspiration, information, and resources useful to enjoying the ride and connecting with local and global cycling communities.

THE OUTCAST
yesweareontheweb.com/outcast/index.html

The art-rock set of the single-speed world.

SAFE ROUTES TO SCHOOLS
www.saferoutestoschools.org

A program spreading across Canada and the US through education and incentives designed to decrease traffic and pollution and increase the health of children and the community by promoting walking and biking to school. The program also addresses the safety concerns of parents by encouraging greater enforcement of traffic laws, educating the public, and exploring ways to create safer streets.

SURFACE TRANSPORTATION POLICY PROJECT
www.transact.org

A diverse, nationwide coalition working to ensure safer communities and smarter transportation choices that enhance the economy, improve public health, promote social equity, and protect the environment.

SUSTAINABLE URBAN TRANSPORT PROJECT
www.sutp.cn/index.php?option=com_frontpage&Itemid=1

A partnership between the German Technical Cooperation, the Bangkok Metropolitan Administration, CITYNET, and the United Nations Economic and Social Commission for Asia and the Pacific that aims to help developing cities achieve sustainable transport goals through international experience and targeted work.

URBAN DEATH MAZE
www.nybma.com

An archive chronicling what might have been the coolest messenger zine of all time.

URBAN VELO
www.urbanvelo.org

A bimonthly Pittsburgh magazine and website reflecting and exploring the everyday cycling culture found in cities. Reader submissions are encouraged.

VELO VISION
www.velovision.co.uk

A website and magazine covering inspired developments in bicycle technology, cycling as transport, and the scope of human power.

VICTORIA TRANSPORT POLICY INSTITUTE
www.vtpi.org

An independent Canadian research organization dedicated to developing innovative and practical solutions to transportation problems.

INDEX

A
Axle skewers, 25–27

B
Barrel adjusters, 65–66, 95–98
Bike riding, virtues and freedom of, 7
Brake cables
    and pad adjustment, 76–77
    and stem adjustment, 53, 56–57
    tightening, 65–66
Brake levers
    and hidden bolts, 60
    tightening, 59–60
Brake pads
    adjusting, 63–65
    adjusting for cantilever brakes, 75–77
    adjusting for disc brakes, 84–85
    adjusting for sidepull brakes, 68–69
    adjusting for V brakes, 80
    cartridge type, 64–65
    and effect of road debris, 66–67
    maximum wear lines, 67
    nonhydraulic rim, 64
    toeing in, 64, 75, 76
Brakes
    adjusting, 63
    BMX U type, 86
    cantilever, 64, 65, 72–77
    cantilever, adjusting centering or
        spring tension, 73–75
    centerpull, 64, 71–72
    checking before riding, 11–12, 43
    coaster, 86
    disc, 67, 81–85

dual-pivot sidepull, 64, 70–71
dual-pivot sidepull, centering, 71
endurance of rim sidewalls, 67
roller, 86
roller-cam, 86
sidepull, 64, 65, 67–70
sidepull, centering, 69–70
V type, 64, 65, 80–81, *82–83*
V type, centering, 77–80

C

Cars, and dangers for bike riders, 7
Cassettes, 35, 36, 90–91
    removing, 36–40, *38–39*
    tools, 33, 36–37
Chainrings, 89
Chains
    bent, 99
    checking before riding, 12–13
    derailleur-caused problems, 94–95

dropped, 103
fixed gear, tightening, 86–87
loose, 103
positioning, 98–99
skipping, 89
tight links, 99–103
Cogs, 89, 90
Cone wrenches, 27
Cranks, 13, 90, 104
    bolts, 104

D

Derailleurs
    adjusting front derailleur, *100–101*
    adjusting rear derailleur, *96–97*
    B-tension screws, 94
    and cable tension, 95–98
    and chain problems, 94–95
    checking alignment, 91–93
    checking before riding, 13

limit screws, 93–95
miscellaneous problems, 104
and reinstalling wheels, 24
Drivetrain
checking before riding, 12–13
checking for adjustments, 89–90
taking care of, 89
See also Cogs; Chains; Derailleurs

F
Flight check, 11–13, 43
"Fourth hand" pliers, 65, 66
Freehubs, 36
Freewheels, 35–36
tools, 33, 35

H
Handlebars
adjusting alignment, 51–52
and brake levers, 59–60

and breakage, 61
checking before riding, 12, 43
and components mounted on, 59–60
See also Stems

P
Pedals, 13, 104

R
Rims, 25
bowed, 30–32
and loose hubs, 28

S
Seatposts
attachment to frame, 47
avoiding removal when parking, 48
avoiding swapping, 47
clamps, 43
maximum height lines, 47

shock posts, 45, 47–48
suspension type, 44, 47, 48
Seats
    checking before riding, 12, 43
    elasticized gel type, 45
    and horizontal alignment, 46
    rails, 43, 46
    saddle height and position, 46–47
    selecting, 45–46
    tightening, 43–45
Spokes
    adjusting, 28–32
    broken, 32–33
    broken, compensating for, 33
    broken, replacing, 33–40
    nipples, 29, 30, 40
    tension, 30, 31, 40
    See also Wheels
Stems
    adjustable, 57–59
    binder bolts, 55

    and breakage, 61
    and cables, 53, 56–57
    expander bolts, 52
    and handlebar alignment, 51–52
    headset bearing adjustment, 54–56
    headsets, loose, 53–54
    headsets, threadless, 54–55
    height adjustment, 53, 56–57
    pivot bolts, 57–59
    preload bolts, 55
    quill, 51, 52–53, 57
    threadless, 51, 56–57
    See also Handlebars

T
Tires
    assessing quality of, 24
    beads, 18–24
    boots, 24–25
    correct pressure, 11
    fixing a flat, 15–24, *16–17, 20–23*

patch kit, 18
removing inner tube, 18
See also Wheels
Tool kit (portable), 7–8

ш

Wheels
bolt-on skewers, 27
checking before riding, 12, 27
flat spots, 31
hops, 31
hubs, loose or tight, 27–28
and lateral play, 27
quick-release axle skewers, 25–27
reinstalling, 24
removing front wheel, 15–18
removing rear wheel, 15, *16–17*
tightening, 25–27
truing (spoke adjustment), 28–32
See also Cassettes; Freehubs;
Freewheels; Rims; Spokes; Tires

Also available from Speck Press

***Bicycle: A Repair & Maintenance Manifesto* by Sam Tracy**